CYBER SAFE

CYBER SAFE

NOLAN BLACKWOOD

publisher logo
Revival Waves of Glory Books & Publishing

CONTENTS

1	Introduction	1
2	Foundations of Cybersecurity	5
3	Securing Your Devices	7
4	Protecting Your Online Identity	9
5	Safe Internet Practices	11
6	Social Media Security	13
7	Mobile Device Security	17
8	Wireless Network Security	21
9	E-commerce Security	23
10	Data Backup and Recovery	25
11	Cybersecurity for Businesses	27
12	Emerging Threats and Trends	29
13	Cybersecurity Laws and Regulations	33
14	Ethical Hacking and Penetration Testing	37
15	Cybersecurity Careers and Training	41
16	Conclusion	45

Copyright © 2024 by Nolan Blackwood
All rights reserved. No part of this book may be reproduced in any manner whatsoever without written permission except in the case of brief quotations embodied in critical articles and reviews.
First Printing, 2024

CHAPTER 1

Introduction

With the increased use of the internet for e-commerce, online banking, and instant communication, the reliance on computers and networks increases every day. This reliance on computers and networks has created fears that hackers, disgruntled employees, and terrorists could damage the nation's critical infrastructure by attacking SCADA systems and possibly taking over process control systems or using SCADA systems from missiles. In the past, the process control systems were proprietary, and security wasn't much of an issue. Today, most companies are switching to open systems protocols to realize the many benefits of these protocols. The standard systems make it much easier to view, track, and trace what is going on in the plant. Hosts can easily see ongoing plant processes. The added benefits open systems protocols have provided aren't without problems.

When the Honeywell TDC 3000 and others like it were best of breed, there were few, if any, standards available for them. The Honeywell protocol, for example, wasn't easily duplicated. Security was much less of an issue when systems used proprietary protocols. Today, most process control vendor protocols are, for better or worse, based on standard open systems protocols. This provides many benefits to a company, enabling it to use many more tools and get a better look at the plant process. It also means security isn't what it used to be. This paper investigates the ability of modern defense mechanisms to protect a SCADA process control system that uses open system protocols. The process control system is expected to withstand an insider who has a multi-tiered organizational role. A hierarchical system design is used to model the expert.

This expert is a user with a top user role on a node on the business network and a bottom node role on a node in the process control network. It is known that the insider would attack other nodes on his network, so a control mechanism tries to limit the damage. The insider expects to be caught, so he attacks a honeynet. The number of tools needed to protect an internal network or SCADA system quickly becomes impractical with the amount of intelligence an expert will have. Just defending will not be enough - at some point, an adversary will obtain the tools needed to walk through modern defense mechanisms.

Understanding the Importance of Cybersecurity

Given this volume of digital information and the way that we create, store, and use it, it is natural that many of us are concerned about our privacy and security in this interconnected world. Despite that, our value-based and control-sensitive concerns about how information about us is being shared online are regularly being ignored by many of the technology and data companies that we use to create, store, and communicate that information. It is quite simple to increase the chances of a positive experience because many of the problems caused by a lack of security have been known for decades. By understanding what it means to be safe online and learning a few basic principles about cybersecurity, we can provide our loved ones and ourselves with an enhanced level of digital life protection.

Every day, each of us creates an enormous amount of personal digital information. Our digital footprint, which includes photos and videos, contact lists and emails, banking information, medical records, and a host of other information about our activities and preferences, is stored in many physical locations around the world. A few organizations, such as email service companies like Google Mail or photo sharing companies like Shutterfly or Facebook, store a very large percentage of the overall digital information. We create and store all this data and information on our own devices or online through the services we use. We capture photos and videos with our mobile phones or digital cameras and share them with friends and family. We work on our desktops and laptops, storing important medical, legal, and financial documentation. Our children spend much of their free time online, and the technology industry knows almost as much about them as we do. Our reliance on this real-time connectivity and data sharing is astounding and is changing the ways in which we do business, interact with one another, and entertain ourselves.

CHAPTER 2

Foundations of Cybersecurity

So, are we taking measures to protect the world's computer systems? Not as much as we should, yet our future depends on it.

While it may be interesting to learn how to write computer programs, understanding and participating in the digital world is important for a far more important reason: the world's infrastructure is controlled by computers, and these computers need to be programmed, maintained, and protected from accidents and attacks. Cars are controlled by computers. Electrical grids are controlled by computers. Nuclear power plants are controlled by computers. Large chemical plants are controlled by computers, as are a large number of buildings. Obviously, military and intelligence systems are also controlled by computers, and are also targets of attack. Even small attacks can have huge effects: a teenager who installed a worm in 2003 that sought to do a modest amount of damage to computers infected tens of millions of machines, leaving some of them permanently ruined.

Basic Concepts and Terminology

Topics range from basic concepts and terminology to the rational defense against complex attack strategies. The defense itself is inseparable from the way systems, software, and services are. Welcome to the twenty-first century. It cannot be said often enough. Everything we rely on calls on more computer software than human technicians understand. Pieces of software written and maintained by clever and hardworking professionals easily number in the billions. Unfortunately, each piece of software, no matter how seemingly trivial its function, is fault-prone and extremely likely to harbor at least a few exploitable vulnerabilities.

This book explains how to protect your digital information - your cyberlife and identity - from harm. Just as importantly, it explains how not to over-protect cyber-lives so that we collectively can utilize the miracle of a hyper-connected world. Safe practice with regard to the way we go about our lives on the web is every bit as crucial as, and frequently inseparable from secure systems and code. Every error, every insufficiently tested assumption, allows the risk that some leg of Internet infrastructure (a switch, router, OS, service, configuration, account permissions, smartphone running Angry Birds) will become the weak link that allows third-party misuse.

CHAPTER 3

Securing Your Devices

When we're extremely familiar or comfortable with something, we can sometimes take it for granted, which can lead us to become complacent. We get into the habit of not paying close attention, of not remaining quite so alert. When we're hardcore fans, for example, of a sports team or movie franchise, we tend to think that we understand or know everything about our beloved subject, and as a result, we might not notice anything else. Unfortunately, context-aware adversaries can take advantage of our complacency or of our blind sides. Suppose an email message were purported to announce an important upcoming game, round, leg or season, or that a link or attachment was labeled as being a song by our favorite artist, or as being a movie about our favorite characters. Might we quickly or carelessly click, download and open? How about a message that told us that we owed even more money and that we needed to confirm our account, and click or open to do so? Would we stop to consider why we were given these just-in-time messages? In-game or real-time notices and popups would be successful because they'd coincide with our current activity.

Best Practices for Computer Security

User training on off-site backup and rapid data recovery (facts) Based on a content analysis of 84 specific security incident investigations, data recovery was the most costly consequence of attacks recently faced by system administrators. Data recovery was cited as a concern more than 50% of the time. Data recovery activities were labeled as disaster recovery or damage control in 93% of the incidents. Data compromises fell into five different non-mutually exclusive categories. The five categories were sabotage, unauthorized use and access, damaged by critical programs, information unavailable, and other concerns. 24% of the incidents resulted in recovery of 4 percent or less recoverable data. Five incidents resulted in recovery of 100% reduced data.

This dissertation has focused on the need for education in the area of computer security. What should be emphasized in the development of educational materials? The following recommendations are based on an analysis of specific security incidents, interviews with professional system administrators, previous research in the areas of user training and management practices, and personal experience. These tests include a combination of user training on offsite backup and efficient data recovery, user training on avoidance of intruders, user and consultant training, full board management, and computer security as an audit concern.

CHAPTER 4

Protecting Your Online Identity

While it's important to protect your computer, tablet, and smartphone with encryption, strong passwords, and two-factor authentication, there's much more to cybersecurity. For one thing, let's be blunt about this: if your identity gets stolen, all that neat cybersecurity will do you little good. You will have been "pwned" big time, no matter how much security is on your computer. Follow these rules to help protect your online identity:

1) Your web browser (Internet Explorer, Mozilla Firefox, Google Chrome, and Apple Safari) has a setting to remember user ID and passwords when logging in to a website. Do not check that box. Yes, it might be a hassle having to remember your login credentials, but allowing your browser to remember your login credentials puts all of your first two authentication factors (something only you should know and something only you should have access to) in one place.

2) Many programs and services have web interfaces that are secured with an encrypted connection, but you can only access the program or service itself (the console from your own computer, smartphone, or tablet) with several single-factor authentications (like a username and password). Do not enable it, or if it is already

enabled, disable Remote Desktop or Remote Management unless you know what you are doing.

Tips for Creating Strong Passwords

To help increase the strength of your passwords, consider getting a password manager. Managers are designed to create, store, update, and even prompt you to change your passwords routinely. With the help of a password manager, you can then have strong, distinct passwords for each of your accounts.

Use at least 10 characters: A longer password is better. Avoid simple words and phrases. Instead, try to mix letters, numbers, and symbols. Try to be unpredictable. The inclusion of numbers, mixed-case letters, and special characters makes a strong password difficult to guess or crack. To make your password harder to guess or crack, try to include three random words. The inclusion of numbers, mixed-case letters, and special characters makes a strong password difficult to guess or crack. Be creative; people who use the same password across different applications are making a hacker's job easy. Keep it secret; don't share your passwords on the phone, in texts or even with family. If your device or favorite application offers a multifactor authentication option, consider using it. Most importantly, recommend a password manager. It will keep a record of all the passwords, allow you to generate new ones that are both strong and distinct, and much more.

Creating a strong and unique password is sometimes easier said than done, but it goes a long way in safeguarding your personal information. To help make it easier for you to develop a well-rounded password security policy, the Federal Trade Commission provides the following tips:

CHAPTER 5

Safe Internet Practices

Other considerations have to be looked at when designing server architecture so that several servers listen on behalf of clients. Occasionally a system is poorly designed and causes a root server file to grow uncontrollably. If the system is a multilateral server, this need not cause a problem, but if the server is a single-site server, then the effect can be bad. Generally, the rule is that when a new function is added to a server, then one is important feedback is needed for the operation of the server; site feedback should be kept to a minimum.

Using good practices when using the internet can save a lot of headaches from cyber criminal activity. A common threat against internet applications is one of Denial of Service (DoS), where an attacker swamps a victim site with requests until it cannot longer function. In some cases, the damage from a DoS attack can extend down the network to include many sites, since an aggregated effect can be far worse than if not aggregate did not occur. An accurate report from the victim site of the bandwidth that should be consumed can be leaked, so we might suggest that some mechanisms are put in place to control the amount of bandwidth used by the server, and then crash the server in another way.

Avoiding Phishing Scams

Two characteristics make phishing scams successful. Many don't require technical exploits in the almost ethereal realm of computer security. They need only the cunning of social engineering, so they can fool any of us. They can infect systems with harmful malware. Such emotional attacks prey upon our behavior. We trust that what is presented to us, like a convincing email, a scary phone call, or even a chance meeting with a person who appears to be locked out of an office and who boxes you into physically letting them in, is true. We may feel that we're in a hurry and not think clearly about it. We may also, unfortunately, be lazy or foolish and not think that scammers can victimize us in this way. We often trust that they are not very interested in doing so. And once the victim has been exploited, the scammer, selling services or information in an anonymous manner, will want to use some of your resources to profit from the trust that you have allowed them to take advantage of.

Phishing is a term used to describe a type of social-engineering attack in which an attacker, commonly through email or instant messaging, masquerades as someone whom the recipient trusts, in order to obtain sensitive information or spread malware or both. Trustworthy disguises, often of trusted brands, make the scams convincing. Urgent and alarmist subject lines are also common. Scam emails may invite victims to click on a link, visit a replica website, and log in, after which their identity and password are compromised. Details of the message, in the form of personal, financial, or other confidential details, may then be requested. Scammers can then use, sell, or give away these details as they please.

CHAPTER 6

Social Media Security

While you are striving to keep strangers from viewing your social media content, some sites and services do offer some level of absolute privacy control over content shared on the site. However, also remember that you should also keep in mind that nothing is completely safe and that comments and information you do not share within a closed private social network can still be subject to some level of compromise. If you do not want a comment seen by a potential employer, spouse, or parent, then do not share it - or even easier, get off social media or block these people. It is hard to share content with everyone if you do not want anyone to know about it.

After you have reviewed your social media accounts and have them posting appropriate private information - keeping someone outside of your friend list from knowing a lot about you from your account - it is time to move to the security and privacy settings of your social media accounts. This is where you can control who can access your profile and who can connect with you. These settings can make your account much more secure and your experience on social media more enjoyable.

Privacy Settings and Data Protection

The progress of technology for the medium of communication is growing fast. An example of the growing technology for the medium of communication is social media. The popularity of social media is attracting many people to follow, like MySpace and LinkedIn. The popularity of Facebook is attracting many people to connect and talk with others. According to consumers, comfort is highly needed during the communication process. The different needs of users about privacy operate on multiple levels. The information is complex and goes beyond asking whether digital privacy exists. The key area of interest that attracted us to the area of privacy in a digital world is the need for privacy settings. Privacy controls are embedded in almost every type of online software, including operating systems, internet browsers, browsers accompanying mobile devices, etc. Control, an essential component of digital privacy, is given acknowledged importance in society. These digital privacy measures are functional means of protecting privacy. With the large amounts of personal information that have been made accessible through websites, it is important to determine not only how much, but what type of private information is available, including one's level of privacy. This digital world often can be optimized to track blueprints, demography, and geography of social relationships and to create them.

Privacy settings: An opportunity to steer and protect the perception of social media. Privacy protection can be viewed through the usage of privacy settings. These settings operate as an underused opportunity within an ongoing process of impression management to steer and, more importantly, protect the perception that is projected onto social media. The more comfort people require, the higher the privacy settings are. The level of privacy settings comes largely from the user. For example, on Facebook, discussion about privacy is going from being very open to closed. There are studies that show that users of Facebook who do not have control over their privacy are likely to disclose less information when it comes to being judged by the employee.

CHAPTER 7

Mobile Device Security

Mobile phones are often loosely secured due to the mistaken thinking that they are inherently secure. Part of the problem is that cellular services are unable to provide the tight security that telcos advertise. To save on costs, mobile voice channels are unprotected from everyone except nosy eavesdroppers without police powers or government-authorized wiretaps – anyone else can easily record confidential conversations. The situation is somewhat better for data transmissions, since data can be encrypted (though it is not clear whether all carriers use encryption for data). Cell towers use strong authentication systems to ensure that only registered phones are allowed to connect, but with the right equipment, a fake base station can sniff out a mobile phone's unique ID number from the air. If you've been involved with sensitive organizations, you know that a technological vulnerability always comes to a bad end! Devices that listen in to and capture cellular conversations are easily available on the commercial market, and both police and civilian lawbreakers use them. Of course, skilled hackers with more resources available can find an even greater variety of tricks to defeat security measures. Cell phone networks use a protocol called Short Message Service to provide store-and-forward shipment of text messages. Unfortunately, the system has no encryption, leading to opportunities for eavesdroppers or miscreants who listen in on SMS traffic and intercept private messages. Because the user control channel has no encryption, a third-string attack creeps in only you! Those who are sneaky can easily obtain a dump of all local cell phone numbers, useful information for spammers and stalkers.

Mobile devices themselves can be threats to security, and new security technologies will need to be developed to meet the risks. Today, mobile device security has many gaps. The leading problem is simply that most people don't use security systems on their mobile devices. We see the evidence of this in two important ways. First, a large percentage of mobile phones are lost. If these phones are not protected with password authentication, the possibility is reality that strangers exploring the menu will find a way to use the phone to access, steal, or destroy information. Second, cell phones are becoming targets of malicious software just as personal computers have been for years. Mobile viruses may not be front-page news today, but since mobile operating systems are based on the same TCP/IP protocol stack that servers and computers work with, they are inevitable. In the same way that the Internet has been forced to develop new security technologies in response to waves of malicious computer software, mobile phone networks may be systematically undermined by floods of infectious code unless reliable security features are designed from the beginning.

Securing Your Smartphone

- Encrypt data and make it invisible. - Be careful when buying or selling a smartphone. - Stay away from internet cafes, public transport kiosks, and public PCs. - Keep wireless carrier specific smartphones out of your travel backpack. - Protect smartphone from GPS tracking and hotspots. - Know that your smartphone is a valuable source of information. - Be smart when traveling abroad. - Buy your own travel cash. - Avoid unnecessary calls home. - When in doubt, always turn it off. - Encrypt your smartphone's hard drive.

Securing your smartphone will help to keep you safe both day and night. From cyber attacks to physical kidnappings, your smartphone is both the key to your information's security and a threat to knowing more than you'd like. Follow these tips to give you the best chance to avoid a potentially dangerous showdown and keep you, your computer, and your smartphone safe. Avoid sending sensitive data from your smartphone, buying a used or rented smartphone, or using public or shared PCs. To prevent tracking or risking reveal your personal data make sure you never make any unnecessary calls home, clean up GPS tagged photos, and encrypt your smartphone's hard drive. As you should with your computer, backup your smartphone often. If possible, do not carry wireless carrier specific smartphones for traveling to foreign countries. Smartphones come in all shapes and sizes. While they may not weigh much, leaving a trail of potentially valuable, potentially dangerous data is the last thing you need.

CHAPTER 8

Wireless Network Security

The default configuration of commercial Wireless Access Points (WAPs) is to provide open Wireless LAN (WLAN) service, allowing any device to connect to the network. The measures needed to secure a Wi-Fi network largely depend on the unique circumstances of the installation. Each owner should carefully weigh the consequences of extra security measures on usability. General principles and guidelines for Wi-Fi security are covered here. Nonprofessionals should consider hiring a network security professional or an independent computer security consultant to do the job. Small businesses may wish to ask neighboring businesses for a recommendation. Up-to-date lists of certified network security professionals are maintained by the Information Systems Audit and Control Association and the international professional association (ISC)2.

Securing your wireless local area network (WLAN) requires understanding the risks and deploying appropriate countermeasures. When deployed properly, Wi-Fi systems can be less risky than wired LANs and provide benefits that are not easily obtainable with their wired predecessors. Poorly deployed Wi-Fi systems, on the other hand, can be fully accessible by anyone with a Wi-Fi radio, far outside the physical boundaries of your premises. Even if they do not know or care about your network, legitimate users of nearby access points may interfere with your Wi-Fi signal, impacting performance and reliability.

Securing Your Wi-Fi Network

Wireless security begins with using the latest encryption standard adopted by your wireless networking device, the Wi-Fi Protected Access Version 3 (WPA3). The original WPA standard is now obsolete and has been replaced. It is also being retired by some Internet Service Providers (ISPs) as WPA is vulnerable to key recovery attack via changing the password on the wireless router. Be sure to secure the router's administrative interface by changing the administrator's user ID to something other than the published default and then setting a strong, unique administrative password. Periodically review the authorized users' list. Most newer wireless routers provide a device list page that shows all devices currently connected to the network. Also check the router's access attempts log as a security measure. These unauthorized access attempts or actual unauthorized accesses are quickly recognizable. Most routers also have the option to save a log file to remote storage, such as a USB drive or network-attached storage (NAS). Cyberattacks are rarely committed over the wireless network, but to prevent concerns, disable the wireless network's administrative user permission.

In this section, we'll cover how to protect your home from pranks, predators, and theft by improving the security of your Wi-Fi network. We will secure both its signal and administrative tools so that you can forget about it.

CHAPTER 9

E-commerce Security

Unlike traditional commerce, however, there are some disadvantages and dangers to e-commerce. Hackers and thieves want access to shoppers' personal and money-related information. These criminals conduct some scams that solely use the Internet, and other sophisticated scams use both the Internet and the telephone.

The prospect of shopping from our homes or offices is certainly attractive. It saves time and money. There is no need to fight traffic, miss meals, fight crowds, or stand in long lines. Online shopping offers a huge marketplace of products. Shoppers are able to choose from among millions of items and receive the goods in record time. One can shop 24 hours a day, seven days a week. Prices are often lower, and shoppers' reviews of items may be read before purchase. Online auctions allow shoppers to bid on rare, one-of-a-kind treasures or buy used items from all over the world. Those who are unable to shop in regular stores, such as the disabled or the elderly, can purchase products online, as can those seeking niche products not stocked in traditional stores.

Safe Online Shopping Practices

Making a physical purchase at a retail store isn't always convenient, which is why many now opt for shopping via the computer.

Using your computer for shopping can save time and gas (you don't even need to leave home for a computer purchase). There are risks that accompany online shopping, and being scammed out of your hard-earned cash or having your financial identity stolen doesn't sound like too much fun. Knowing what can happen and knowing the safeguards to protect yourself can enable you to shop confidently.

Learn the risks that accompany online shopping and the procedures for a safe transaction.

Book Contents: 1: Cyber Predator: Protecting Your Family, Friends, and Yourself Online 2: Defending Your Identity: Preparation and Deflection of Phishing Attacks 3: Parental Security: Safety Online, Making Your Home a Fortress 4: Good Practice in Cyber Warfare Defense in Depth 5: Hardware Trojan Threat, Damage Assessment and Risk Management 6: Protecting the Value Using the Information Fuzzy-SLD in Public-Private Partnership on Cyber Security 7: Ransomware Countermeasures for the Enterprise 8: Reducing Online Reputation Risk: Guides for a Safer Career, Social and Love Life Through Safe Social Media Practices 9: Safe Online Shopping Practices 10: School-Based Internet Safety Curricula and Prevention Programs in the USA 11: The Relevance and Implementation of Cyber Security Policies 12: US University Students' Perceptions of Law Enforcement and Application Security in Online Shopping

CHAPTER 10

Data Backup and Recovery

Backup strategy is a large component of all levels of data recovery. It's also complex and difficult to plan. Be just as concerned with how to restore your backups as backing up your data. Start with the premise that a hard disk failure will occur in the future. Next, consider why and how you would recover, and in what sequence. Strive to include plans in your strategy regarding your boot partition or drive (critical system files). As we store a large amount of data on our PCs, the most common backup media are hard disks and portable disk drives. Another view is to use multiple hard drives within the computer. Normally only one hard drive is used in a PC. Compare and contrast the use of multiple drives.

With the amount of data that many of us store on our systems these days, it's just a matter of time before our hard drives will crash and we lose vital information. Sometimes it's those precious personal photographs you've taken, and sometimes it's your company's files containing orders, clients, or financial figures. In many cases, we overlook the importance of keeping backup copies of our critical data... until it's too late. This chapter explores data backup and recovery issues and suggests different storage media and strategies to recover losses sooner than later.

Importance of Regular Backups

The backup should also be automated so that you do not lose valuable data if you forget to create a copy. This automation process should be set up only with caution, in case, for example, you accidentally rename the files that you are working on. Finally, your hard drive needs to be fire-resistant and the data has to be encrypted. In the event of a fire, your data won't be lost, but if the drive is unencrypted, you may lose it anyway in a completely different way. As we've already noted, some malware can recognize external hard drives, seek out, and encrypt stored user files. These drives may also be stolen, as they are a popular target for thieves.

If you can afford only one safety measure, buy an external backup hard drive. This is the easiest and cheapest way to protect yourself from all kinds of virus attacks and software malfunctions that could lead to loss of data stored on your computer. Backing up data is a crucial component of cybersecurity too, as many new types of malware encrypt the targets' files with a private key, making recovery impossible unless you pay your cyber-extortionist for the corresponding decryption key. Antivirus programs that perform real-time scanning of filesystem operations will offer some mitigation, but an external backup drive will do a much better job.

CHAPTER 11

Cybersecurity for Businesses

The most common enterprise security breach is the one most of us are familiar with: the repurposing of login names and passwords that grant access to sites that have nothing to do with work. It's the corporate blight that visits a host of popular websites, not a redefinition of your own business's data-triage policy. When employees use the same passwords at work and away from work (a habit the password managers we looked at earlier can help you break), hackers are often able to enter the network by trying out the information on their own websites. Ugh. Employees use terrible, terrible passwords. To help them shore up this part of the company's defenses, consider a service like LastPass. (You could help everyone keep their passwords a secret by enrolling in one of the identity-theft protection plans outlined in earlier chapters, too).

Hackers favor businesses as targets because the data they handle is usually more valuable than what consumers can provide. A single stolen credit card might fetch only a few dollars on the black market. The contents of a company's internal database, on the other hand, could yield millions in profits. Corporations and other organizations also must store sensitive data on tons of people: employees, customers, clients, consultants, vendors. Therefore, they represent a massive vulnerability in the battle against cybercrime.

Protecting Company Data

Does cybersecurity really matter to me?

I work in a big company. Protecting company data is someone else's responsibility. I can't do much about it, so why should I care?

In this interconnected world, protecting company data is everyone's responsibility. The amount of data collected (electronically) or produced and shared by companies is staggering. Credit card information, Social Security numbers, passport data, driver's license information, all in the aggregate. Studies have shown that employees' email addresses are 65% exposed online, and only 53% of employees have passwords for their office systems.

Employees play an important role in keeping data secure. For example, think about the countless interactions you have at work and the documents you produce or review. A careless and untrained workforce at any one of these steps could prove costly. Employees and contractors are often the first line of defense in protecting the company's secure data.

Metadata removal is an important practice to help mitigate risk. People are that strong link in mitigating that risk. Can you imagine losing your email list to unsolicited spam and potential phishing? Keep it private!

Lastly, protect data for the good of the company and your job security. Ransomware is a growing threat as the "business model" is so profitable. At least one major company has paid a seven-figure ransom and another spent $15 million on a security assessment project. However, the cost in lost customers', reputation, and goodwill should not be underestimated. If you work for a company that loses sensitive data, someone's head likely will roll, right?

CHAPTER 12

Emerging Threats and Trends

Devices are connecting to the Internet in new and fascinating ways. The Internet of Things (IoT) has resulted in fridges which can reorder your groceries or smart cars that can minimize your risk of crashing. It has also grown the number of Internet-connected devices, where a cyber assailant can stage a massive distributed denial-of-service (DDoS) attack on the infrastructure we rely on daily for work and pleasure. And let's not forget ransomware; this low-cost, high-profit method of making an easy buck is here to stay. As time moves inexorably forward, we can count on novel threats entering this digital world through the doors that technological progress has wrought. While you might not be able to afford a top-end next-generational firewall from Cisco, there are items you can add to your back-end Internet security systems to prevent new waves of cyber attacks. In this chapter, we will examine a broad variety of new threats that we as information technology (IT) professionals are going to need to shore up against.

The use of technology is evolving at such a rapid pace that it is hard to stay current on new dangers, such as widespread smartphone hacking or Android malware. In this modern digital era, we are all interconnected in so many ways that the tiniest cyber misstep can have catastrophic results. We are way beyond the point where we could simply say, "It can't happen to me." Our computers, laptops, and smartphones are gateways with access to our contacts, appointments, emails, and other important files. While our smart devices and consumer electronics can add convenience to our lives, they also add another layer of objects found in homes, offices, and schools that can be compromised by an outsider. We need to lock these gateways.

Ransomware and Cryptojacking

Earlier in this chapter, I talked about one well-advertised form of pop-up mining called Coinhive. Coinhive is legitimate mining software provided by the developers of the Monero cryptocurrency. Over 90 percent of all legal uses of Coinhive are for mining Monero on web servers. Legitimate Coinhive usage involves putting a small JavaScript script into a web page shown to a user. When a user presses their browser's "view" button, they activate the script, causing their browser to spend cycles running the script and mining Monero for the Coinhive developers. Websites using Coinhive typically display a notification on their site and an indirect arrangement with their users. Ransomware creators have flipped Coinhive from a voluntary offering to a malware business model. This combination is called cryptojacking.

In recent years, ransomware has taken the cybersecurity community by storm. A kind of malware, ransomware locks down its victims' files using strong encryption and only decrypts them in exchange for payments, typically valued in Bitcoin, of hundreds or thousands of dollars. Ransomware can spread using a broad variety of attack vectors including phishing, drive-by downloads, exposed remote desktop services, and software vulnerabilities. As soon as it encrypts a victim's files, ransomware presents a screen, window, or message either instructing the victim who to contact or directing them to make payments over the Tor anonymity network. The basic goals of ransomware are to encrypt data, extort money, and get paid, often through the proxy of a tumbler.

CHAPTER 13

Cybersecurity Laws and Regulations

To obtain a sense of the prevalence of this class of breach, the Secret Service questioned 110 service providers in 2003. Its report found that bad employees or former employees were the most common threat, involved in 59% of cases, often in concert with other entities. The question is founded on evidence that about one-quarter of the 504 breaches reported since 2005 have been the result of intentional hacking or insider sabotage (including theft and unintended mishaps).

The first version of the Data Accountability and Trust Act (DATA), H.R. 2221, was reintroduced in Congress in July 2009. Three key factors inform concerns about the current patchwork of state laws: the growing incidence of breaches, the effect they are having on victims, and the extent to which regulatory inconsistency adds to companies' compliance costs.

For years, consumer advocates have argued for national legislation to require that breached organizations notify victims of information theft. In 2005, 17 states imposed varying security and notification regulations on organizations holding personal information.

There are many existing laws and regulations at both the federal and state levels that apply to certain activities in cyberspace. When dealing with computer and network security, it is important for businesses and individuals to be aware of these laws and regulations. However, it should be noted that while these laws are designed to ensure that organizations protect certain types of information, such as consumer credit card and medical details, they are only minimum standards.

Compliance and Data Protection Laws

No single data protection or privacy law is comprehensive enough to meet the requirements of every country. The laws are designed to work in cooperation with other laws and with effective business practices. Therefore, avoiding conflicts with differing business compliance requirements presents a significant challenge to any organization doing business on the Internet that requires access to personal information from both employees and customers around the world. As always, you should become familiar with the data protection and privacy laws with which your organization must comply and the various "best practice" guidelines designed to assist in doing so.

A significant and growing number of countries around the world have adopted or are preparing to adopt new data protection and privacy regulations. To provide for the free flow of personal information across borders, discussions are underway among governments, businesses, and other organizations on achieving harmonization of data protection laws. Microsoft is helping to lead the way in these discussions by participating in numerous international data protection and privacy organizations and initiatives, and by encouraging the adoption of fair information privacy practices. The European

Union Data Directive is a good example of international cooperation to protect individual privacy.

CHAPTER 14

Ethical Hacking and Penetration Testing

Security testing is the process to assess the solution's current level of security. In this process, examination is done by applying various testing techniques. In layman's terms, security can be described as how resistant the information is to loss. Security should emphasize the authenticity, availability, non-repudiation, reliability, and integrity of data. Considering all the requirements, a new method called penetration testing, also known as ethical hacking, was developed. The basic purposes of penetration testing are to locate vulnerabilities and to simulate an attack against a large Internet-based system. The main goal of penetration testing is to provide a better security environment and assistance for secure functional capabilities. Ethical hackers manage all types of risks being exposed to the real class of sensitive data within the data center. These sensitive data can include hands-on skills in transactions, configuration information, customer-specific databases, and customer-confidential paper regarding services. Their goal is to exploit identified vulnerabilities, circumvent security controls, and perform discovery testing requests related to the identified e-commerce data environment.

The main objectives of this chapter are: - To introduce the concepts of ethical hacking. - To give an introduction to the tools and techniques used by ethical hackers.

The most important aspect of information security is to evaluate and review the security level of existing or planned solutions. Failure to evaluate the security of these solutions can contribute to a weakened or non-secure system. Reviewing the security of the solution can prevent the loss of sensitive or critical information. Ethical hacking is a way to review the solution by using the skills and tools used by real hackers. Prior information about hacking will be helpful for carrying out ethical hacking. This chapter will give an introduction to ethical hacking and the tools and techniques that are used.

Understanding White-Hat Hacking

We believe recognition and certification of the professional white-hat hacker belonging to the security community is founded on the basis of improvements in stability, security, and reliability, whether on behalf of the general public or private organizations, of networked infrastructure, systems, and end products. Such a positive perception may include corporations hiring certified individuals to help them pen-test their networks in the face of active security infrastructure defenses (at minimum expense). Moreover, networked software will have been hack-tested in controlled environments.

The justification for introducing a certifiable white-hat hacking curriculum and ethical hacking test begins by pointing out that hacking is already pervasive throughout the hacker community and a large fraction of existing security professionals. A costly arms race between illicit hackers and internal defense has existed in which hackers amuse themselves by finding new vulnerabilities in sites at the expense of organization and corporate security infrastructures. The NIDS, NIPS, and Antivirus industries are well-documented ongoing multibillion-dollar industries. For years, "hacking" has been frowned upon as an unofficial activity, something IT security professionals do not maliciously obtain access to a sensitive network or devices. However, hacking, in an ethical fashion, would benefit many of these same organizations.

The idea of a certified "ethical hacking" program seems to generate widely divergent viewpoints. While some may view ethical hacking as a joke or a contradiction, we believe there are many individuals who wish to certify their technical skills in a white-hat hacking profession. We further believe that there are many individuals who are called upon by their employers on a regular, if informal, basis to assume this responsibility. Individuals who perform testing of their own organization's networks, or within the scope of explicitly authorized pen-testing programs, now have a means by which they can certify their skills before independent industry.

CHAPTER 15

Cybersecurity Careers and Training

For those of you who have been enlisted or are planning to enlist in military service, cybersecurity is an attractive alternative as a post-service career. Even if you are currently thinking about information technology (IT) or computer science specialties such as computer hardware maintenance, server management, software development, website design, network management for the likes of Microsoft, Cisco, or Red Hat configurations, help desk support, or program management at startup companies in the technology industry, cybersecurity plays an enabling cross-disciplinary role in the support professions. At no other time in history has the demand for the qualifications for cybersecurity job openings ever been more prominent. Small wonder computer security education and cybersecurity technical capacity training are continually at the forefront of the United States on-the-job and education and training directives.

Even the most inexperienced of technology users are well aware of the career opportunities centering on computer-related skills, and that demand is not slowing down. In fact, a quick search online finds hundreds of thousands of unfilled positions related to cybersecurity jobs throughout the country, jobs are in critical need of hiring.

As more individuals and corporations come to rely on the Internet and cyberspace, products and services need to be created that protect from attack any more fiscal, reputational, and physical infrastructure, which is why cybersecurity careers, for the most part, have such high percentage rates for salaries and job openings. Whether you are a new college graduate or a mid-career professional looking for a career change, chances are that you have been, are now, or will be considering a career in cybersecurity.

Paths to a Career in Cybersecurity

Traditional university programs concentrating on computer security are growing everywhere, but are not yet enough. Although most important computer security areas have been in plain view for twenty years, there are few people who have deep enough knowledge of the tools and philosophy of security to design, review, find loopholes in, or implement a system or network that will interface them without danger. Both corporations and universities are currently having trouble filling their ranks (in teaching, research, or applied work) with known good computer security people by the normal hiring mechanisms. This is partly because there's less than half of one good job seeker available for every good job at this writing, but mainly because most of those available are widely distributed and are already employed.

Once you get caught up in hacking, computer security, or cryptography, you may feel that you've found the work you were born to do. Not everyone feels that way, but many engineers, consultants, computer scientists, and writing students do. The job market is incredibly attractive too. There are currently approximately 200,000 positions in the United States that require a heavy focus on cybersecurity, and 30,000 or 40,000 jobs in computer security are going begging worldwide at any time. Salaries for good people have risen and risen over the last ten years; they always will, as long as the need for computer security grows explosively.

CHAPTER 16

Conclusion

Using a credit card, which won't care about it themselves, would seem a lot safer than using a debit card or cash. The large insurance company headquartered in the United States avoids the international fund transfers, the ones which carried the highest fees. It also realizes that transferring money to an unfamiliar bank or unfamiliar "service" may be riskier, and thus more likely to produce claims, than working through a detailed relationship formed after accepting money from the other organization. Unfortunately, people often come up with the money for extras item when the item was never a profitable investment.

In the end, keeping your life safe in a digital world really isn't very different from other eras. It's all about thinking through what you do and managing the risks. People past the sixth grade should not be passing along each and every email in their inbox with chain letters full of "amazing" stories or unsupportable warnings. Probably neither their friends nor their jobs are absolutely dependent on them reading the snake oil stories and other half-truths trying to make it through them - they probably ought to make better, more selective decisions about what they spend their time reading. Buying "extras" items, particularly from a place where one hasn't done business before, requires a little more care than it takes to buy groceries at the supermarket or buy a book from.

Summary of Key Points

If being cyber safe is so important to so many of us, how can we make sure that everyone who needs to can be safe? It all starts with the individuals who themselves engage in safe – hopefully safe – practices and activities. Governments and organizations also play a role in enabling cyber safe practice – setting social policies, funding support services, and working closely in partnership with communities to provide the necessary support to enable everyone to access cyberspace and be safe.

By now, it should be evident that being cyber safe is not just for one group of people in society. It's not just for those with knowledge of computers or those who are really 'plugged in' to the virtual world. Being cyber safe is the responsibility of everybody in the community. Increasingly, we are all becoming interconnected in the virtual world – whether we want to be or not! But many people – and especially the most powerless, such as children and the elderly who are easily exploited – are left behind through a lack of knowledge or access.

www.ingramcontent.com/pod-product-compliance
Lightning Source LLC
LaVergne TN
LVHW041638070526
838199LV00052B/3443